ZODIAC OF ECHOES

ZODIAC OF ECHOES

Khaled Mattawa

AUSABLE PRESS
2003

Cover art: Balqees Fakhro
"Birth" (detail), acrylic on canvas.
Collection of the artist.

Design and composition by Ausable Press.
The type is Van Dijck with Felix Titling.
Cover design by Rebecca Soderholm.

Published by
AUSABLE PRESS
1026 HURRICANE ROAD
KEENE NY 12942
www.ausablepress.com

Distributed by
Small Press Distribution
800-869-7553
www.spdbooks.org

The acknowledgments appear on page 107 and constitute
a continuation of the copyright page.

Library of Congress Cataloging-in-Publication Data
Mattawa, Khaled 1964—
Zodiac of echos : poems / by Khaled Mattawa.
p. cm.
ISBN 1-931337-04-7 (hardcover : alk. paper)
ISBN 978-1-931337-16-8 (pbk. : alk. paper)
I. Title.

PS3563.A8387Z44 2003
811'.54—dc21
2003013779

for M

ALSO BY KHALED MATTAWA

Poetry:
Ismailia Eclipse
The Sheep Meadow Press, 1995

Translations:
Hatif Janabi, *Questions and Their Retinue: Selected Poems*
University of Arkansas Press, 1996

Fadhil al-Azzawi, *In Every Well A Joseph Is Weeping*
Quarterly Review of Literature, 1997

Saadi Youssef, *Without An Alphabet, Without A Face:*
Selected Poems, Graywolf Press, 2002.

Anthology:
Post Gibran: New Arab American Writing (co-editor)
Syracuse University Press, 1999.

ZODIAC OF ECHOES

ECHO & ELIXIR 1

It shines through clouds and rain.
It dyes the streets with its pink blossoms.
The day crawls through its tunnels.
The roads are long and long.

City without words. Night without night.
Somewhere I remember
these clothes are not my clothes.
These bones are not my bones.

I forget and remember again.
Ships in the harbor which is the sea
which is the journey
that awakens a light inside my chest.

Look at the hands turning the knobs.
The hands that haul the machine.
The man on the phone calling,
hanging up, calling again.

Dust and twisted nails, pebbles
and pieces of broken china,
and all the sweeping that goes on in the world.
No help.

No use saying "I will wait."

It flowers into decades of May.
It shines the windows with your passing gaze.

1.

THE ROAD FROM BILOXI

Qader blew at a cigarette, stuck his head
out the window. Carol wondered why she left,
was beginning to see living in peace
with the rebels that took her father's ranch.
My brother and I up front wondered why
we hadn't killed each other all these years.
We were stuck on the Biloxi highway, mid-July,
the AC kaput, and what the radio played
didn't matter, Randy Travis on the rise,
the days of disco a bruised heap, Reagan,
Meese, Jane Fonda, and the gain in the pain.
Of course, we all felt like burning American flags
on behalf of a thousand justifiable causes.
But who cares? We were stuck for hours,
stuck in 1982, and what blocked the way didn't matter,
and the sea we went to see was no big deal,
a great disappointment in fact, an ocean
brow-beaten by a river, rumbling, moaning
black-eyed, bruised, weighed by Mississippi silt.
And the salty air we came to breathe
did not appear, only swamp algae
and the death smell of moss, the slime,
the invisible webs that trapped ghosts
in lukewarm water, the dead who would not dissolve—
Tom Sawyer, not dissolving, Huck Finn
not dissolving, Big Jim not dissolving,
Goodman, Chaney, Medgar not dissolving,
Cherokee tears floating on top like drops of oil,
Lakotas still streaming down, Kiowas
still coming down, Sioux still floating,
still in the Mississippi where everything seemed

tenuous, everything seemed it would revert back
to the dreams of sickly pale men and women,
back to the nightmares of runagates and domestics,
all hanging there, in the air over Biloxi,
clinging to crayfish and the gnarled hands of shrimpers.
It hovered ominous, a poisonous lethargy
not far from the town we lived in, which God knows
did not matter, making tomorrow matter even less
as long as we were here the week after and the month.
Next time, we promised, it'll be the Atlantic, next time
some salty immensity, some honest to goodness breeze,
the smell of the earth turning around itself,
a clear run to the horizon, a clean shot to Africa,
to something we could beckon and understand,
something the waves would release us from
now that we were stuck here on the Biloxi road
chained, and chain smoking, aware of the sea
we left behind, and that had left us,
the Mediterranean, that other swamp, too far
to touch us again, too far to ever matter.

ECHO & ELIXIR 2

Cairo's taxi drivers speak to me in English.
I answer, and they say your Arabic is good.
How long have you been with us? All my life
I tell them, but I'm never believed.
They speak to me in Farsi, speak to me in Greek,
and I answer with mountains of gold and silver,
ghost ships sailing the weed-choked seas.
And when they speak to me in Spanish,
I say Moriscos and Alhambra.
I say Jews rescued by Ottoman boats.
And when they speak to me in Portuguese,
all my life I tell them, coffee, cocoa,
Indians and poisoned spears.
I say Afonsso king of Bikongo writing
Manuel to free his enslaved sons.
And Cairo's taxi drivers tell me
your Arabic is surprisingly good.
Then they speak to me in Italian,
and I tell them how I lay swaddled
a month's walk from here. I tell them
camps in the desert, barbed wire, wives
and daughters dying, camels frothing disease,
the sand stretching an endless pool.
And they say so good so good.
How long have you been with us?
All my life, but I'm never believed.
Then they speak to me in French,
and I answer Jamila, Leopold, Stanley,
baskets of severed hands and feet.
I say the horror, battles of Algiers.
And they speak to me in English

and I say Lucknow, Arbenz. I say indigo,
Hiroshima, continents soaked in tea.
I play the drum beat of stamps. I invoke
Mrs. Cummings, U.S. consul in Athens,
I say Ishi, Custer, Wounded Knee.
And Cairo's taxi drivers tell me
your Arabic is unbelievably good.
Tell the truth now, tell the truth,
how long have you been with us?
I say my first name is little lion,
my last name is broken branch.
I sing "Happiness uncontainable"
and "fields greening in March"
until I'm sad and tired of truth,
and as usual I'm never believed.
Then they lead me through congestion,
gritty air, narrow streets crowded with
Pepsi and Daewoo and the sunken faces
of the poor. And when we arrive, Cairo's
taxi drivers and I speak all the languages
of the world, and we argue and argue about
corruption, disillusionment, the missed chances,
the wicked binds, the cataclysmic fares.

RAIN SONG
After Al-Sayyab

The radio blares "Dialogue of Souls,"
and the woman who hated clouds
watches the sky.
Where is the sea now? she asks.
Where is it from here?
What is its name?—
this rain on a morning ride to school,
winter, my seventh year,
my father driving
through rain, his eyes fixed on a world
of credit and debt. On the
radio, devotion to
the lifter of harm from those who despair,
knower of secrets with the knowledge of certainty.
Not even the anguish of those
years, the heavy
traffic, cold and wind could have
touched me. I was certain the palm
holding me would be
struck again. Chance allows
for that and for stars to throb
in reachable depths.
Filled with grief bordering happiness,
I didn't care if I was safe,
whether the storm
was over, only that it came, the slash
of lightning, the groaning sky,
and the storms we made,
how rain stripped everything of urgency,
how to the lifter of harm rise
those who despair.

We have returned to your shade.
We have turned to you for rain.
            And a king leads
        his nation in prayer. Thousands stand
behind him. When he bows on a silk
            carpet, his subjects
        follow. Their words are gutters that moan
in the rain. Behind them the sea
            flops its belly,
        the sea stroked by the hand of nightfall
where a sobbing flares, and wind.
            It's coming now
        to make the ground speak in whispers
of mist, moonbeams on a riverbed
            lightening, tense
        lines on an angry brow, and the self
is lost, as if in Nebraska—
            driving through
        flashflood storms. Omaha, Lincoln,
and kingdoms of corn and wheat
            smitten by the field
        mice's helplessness and the silence of birds
in the trees. Darkness rushes
            in its black ambulance
        shepherding dread. I pray because
there is no shelter from floating
            on a sea of distances,
        forgetting that I was raised where rain
meant fire, children fussed over,
            and the songs they sang
        were the oars that broke the first shadows

of dawn, forgetting how
           the engines that spurted
        across the bay sifted through
the water's dreams, shredding
           seaweed, erasing
        my city's blood stained slates.

Go now, measure the solitude
           of a man walking
        in the rain. Comfort the woman who hated
clouds as she looks out
           her window, her chest
        a sponge rain soaks with despair.
Beckon the sea buried in night
           to rise and listen
        to prayers brushed with silk, prayers
on parched lips, and the creaking
           ruts, the whistling
        pipes, gullies and ravines broken-
boned where the chant of a thousand
           wailers blares.
        Go now, pouring rain, bless my
friends walking through
           a storm. A ritual
        follows. Towels, a pinch of salt
and swigs of rum. They remember
           their island homeland.
        Bliss to them is the sound of rain,
its lascivious dancing, its steel-
           hulled pulse,
        its sugar stained bacchanal. And the homeless

woman who storms into a store
               in Indiana; no one
         is startled by her stagger, or the wisps of hair
that line her forehead, as if
         all is forgiven,
        for now, in the rain. And the Mississippi sun,
for hours on end an iron-
            press turning
      roads into mush, and the lingering licorice
scent of tar. Afternoon
          clouds hurl
      half-dollar drops of rain at windshields.
Skirts of steam swirl
         and veil storefronts
      and trees. Bless me now pouring
rain as the world I know
         leaves me,
      the swords that pierced the sky unsheathed
and clanking, thongs of mud
        across the road.
      And the city opens its eyelids of rain,
its vision of dull embers
         fixed within me.

ECHO & ELIXIR 3

Cigarettes in the bar, a beer,
the odyssey ends with a boarding pass.
In the duty-free shops, does one buy
perfume or Tunisian dates?
People do not ask how long you've been away,
but what have you brought?
And being away is all you bring.
Trepidation fills your shoulder bag,
and the ache writes a book of coffee
grinds and your mother's bread.

I've been reading Plato looking for a word.
Dirt reddens and browns, yellows and grays.
Abdulhamid the Scribe, Barthes, Fanon,
Abdulrahman Falcon of Quraish.
Gilgamesh still on his boat waiting
to land on beaches full of people who wait.
In your absence, there is no avoiding legend,
yet you are still a child.
Sappho and Khansa taught you that.
And the life in the hands you shake,
the poetry in the sand more than the poetry in poetry.

I am a spirit and a body.
The trees speak a language of light and thorns.
Let me tell you a story now.
You see a city in the clouds
and give it a woman's name,
always a woman's name.
Let me tell you about my loved one's hair.
You take a blade of grass
and for a second
you are a citizen of its taste.

FOR YEARS I'VE BEEN PROHIBITED
FROM MENTIONING THE MOON

So now the cedar-scented moon, and moon-
glow encasing the sky in lavender velvet,
clouds splotched on a moon-radiant sky
and a sickle moon raking a field of violets
and the moon and sun in Joseph's dream kneeling,
and how years ago we could've been on the moon
watching the city from an airplane,
the stadium lights a diamond necklace,
and she was there, a star singing,
but we wished to be back on earth to know
the measure of our loss, to see
a star singing, her voice drifting beyond
a necklace of light filling the city's dim streets.
How many times, though for years I've been barred
from mentioning the moon, how many times
have I switched off the lights to gaze at the sky,
the moon full or receding, holding court,
how the breeze itself changed the light,
how I wanted to weep at the sight of the moon rising
from the hills of Indiana brightening a frozen stream?
How many times have I turned into this subdivision,
the pipes stacked like a tangle of pythons,
the fire hydrant, tall as a man, exposed, its lower pipes
to be buried under pavement and sick lawns?
I know this hour, the thick lament to come,
the thousands churned. I know this laughter
tearing at my lungs, because seeing the moon
is no consolation for what was to be lost.
But here's what really happens: I see the moon

surrounded by the rubble of conquest
where there are only old stars and dead wolves,
and I am moved again by something I felt before,
shaken, but without an atom of pity in my body,
filled with a transparency capable of bearing
the whole world, a void that takes in the moon
in the sky, the pipes and the evil they gush,
and the poisoned water, and the lead-laced dirt.
Only the moon and whatever spins within me
as I worship all that remains, each speck of light,
every crooked ray beaming from my chest.

THE WIND

It wraps me in night walks.
It calls a name I always assume
to be mine. It announces the trees
and lets the birds in on her secret.
The wind that blows through my window
is the same wind that blows through theirs.
Some have chimes to receive it,

some spice it with their food,
some use it to carry their music
and pelt the sidewalks with its thuds.
And some, like me, let it blow through
the hall and out the kitchen door.
The same wind, the same force
that binds and severs.

*

I am on the phone with Jonathan.
I stand by the window so he can see me,
and he's on the sidewalk waving.
What joy the philosopher, my friend, has
in his body! We're connected, stretching
our voices to a common warehouse
among the stars, our words sorted out

and sent back down to us by something
not unlike the wind that belongs to no one.
We might as well have been two boys
talking through cans and string,
a mystery we wrought that is wholly ours.
But we are trusting the wind now,
or something like it, a force of others.

*

Mr. Stevens, the men born of the sun,
the ones who willed their disavowal to
inscripted currents, are now rural pagans,
school teachers, half-educated, mostly bored,
men and women who've surrendered
to sorceries and knighthoods approachable
only by the tongue's softest syllables.

The woman who slackened off her worship
is now slackening to oblivion, the sound
of a weed whacker, the sound of a snow plow.
She is beyond choice now.
We plunged with her in the green
of her parakeet, walked through climates
more pungent than her oranges.

The bird's colors she'd spread over canvas,
the pleasure of licking her fingers—
the act's finesse, not its seed of wonder—
etched by immeasurable hands on totem poles
made of new lumber. Now it's the buzz
of others, unearthly, that fills her air.
She is not dead. She cannot stop dying.

*

Whitman did not know he knew. He praised
what he grew to condemn. And you knew
what spread beyond your grasp.

A supreme resistance, yours tile-like,
meticulous, oddly arranged. His in wide hacks
into the medium of the air. Now geometry
marshals us to arrivals marked by milestones

of human nerves.
                        Shall I wake "hunger"
from his sleep? Shall I raise the ghosts
of ancient abstractions to define us, to tell us
our names? We all improvise, our chimes,
our spices, our annulments of silence. It dries
our clothes, carries our scents roiling with others',
in democracy, in the spirit of confluence.

★

Jonathan, Mr. Stevens, is still on the phone
waving from the sidewalk. He sees
my silhouette in the window frame. He is
talking to a silhouette in a window frame.
And I am talking to a man standing
on the sidewalk setting time for dinner.
We are held by will and chance, an enigmatic

mesh, but not wholly unimaginable.
Our words, his hands adding stress
to his vowels, the aftertaste
in a West Virginia persimmon
a woman picked and offered me,
a delectable sorrow, intractable:
our bittersweet insistence.

2.

VICINITY
(A Sequence)

I.

An artificial heart whirs,
the patient
a splitting image—   our first ancestor
falling to famine,   and below the cut,

subway cars plunge into the sea
"to form a reef
                    off the Delaware shore."

What do you mean to me now
that I have become your substance?
You a moment
                    and I am your duration,
a web of instincts   refined
        toward a pure savagery,
                            paradisal, pubescent.

Sunlight singes the yard.
Meteorologists pant
                    "a record streak
of hundred degree weather."
Drought sends mountain lions and black bears
        into towns
                    hunting for food.

A policy of state assassination   "is given
the green light" again—
                    the unearthly become inadvertent:

the pulse of the continent
                    throbbing through the metal desk.

"Verily the Lord hath not made a man
                            with two hearts in his chest."
"Verily, beloved, the hearts in this heart
                            chant your name."

The ballpoint threatens
                    to carve it
                                on the totem pole,
        to prod the faces
                    that betray   nothing.

II.

A millionth of an ounce of plutonium

A political gesture: immigrant snivel . . .

                        can cause cancer.

I still have to trust a subtle tenderness
to see
        the worn, the fallen,
                    a ragged star, a sign.

Two electricians lost their larynxes to throat cancer.
Workers handled 100,000 tons
                        of plutonium-laced uranium

recycled from Hanford's

                spent reactor fuel.

I didn't know, didn't believe,

                  only an urge: a conduit
propelled out of a sky touched by its own emptiness
       until something human comes.

The government does not know
how much of the material flowed
through the plant
           from the 1950's to the '70's.

Why don't you go away, and take
your historical antagonism with you . . .
Woman and boyfriend—
the centaur, reared in burial grounds

                     or story books,
the dream caught in the willow draping them—
are charged with injury to her 18-month-old child.

Questioning the air, one fast,

             last time,
I sought a bequeathal,

       a swirl.

★

VICTORIAN VILLAGE

They sit on porches spitting tobacco juice.
They sniff at the children of Narcissus.

Their Saabs of cocksuck.
Their Lexus of hair removal products.

Refugees boned of anemia,
choked by pawn shops and coal dust.

Their TV's blaring all day long,
their ecclesiastes, their classic rock.

Ringed by the fist (spread your legs)
the flashing light, probation officer,

social worker on Thorazine,
the priest in the pink of health,

the midnight evangelist and his snakes,
Jenny and her nights on the streets,

Chuck and his schizophrenia,
Jim and his lottery fix.

And Mama Jean (her chihuahua barking
out in the yard) welcomes them all.

Her ham hock, her split pea soup,
her biscuits, her American cheese.

★

A few weeks ago I was with old school friends when we heard a ruffling in the poinciana nearby. We dismissed it and continued our talk. I hadn't seen those two since high school, and after glossing over their 8 years in jail for "conspiracy," they delved into the future, an internet café, unlimited hours, troubleshooters making house calls, and a 24-hour hot-line (if the phone lines ever work, they joked). Then a cat emerged out of the tree, grasping in its jaws a dove hardly smaller than itself. We watched it traipse across a fence top studded with shards of broken glass.

What my friends could have said sank beyond our wits. They looked exhausted and I sensed my privilege. Our differences bore their weight against us until, at last, a breeze blew. The leaves and branches shivered as if to rid themselves of what had just happened among them. I asked about another schoolmate. "He's an officer at Internal Security," said one of my friends. "A big cat over there."

III.

To shore up an unwillingness,
the moon sinks, takes my questions with it.

Accustomed now,
                    loss and the expectation,
pebbles flung at my hide.

Night falls, its apparitions a host of hungers
sounded in revved-up engines, whoops, sirens, smashed glass
and all the other contraptions of rescue, to rescue . . .

Walking the neighborhood,
                what dusk light I gather
                                lodges within me.

  A confident inhale:

"In professional sports,"
        (a vortex of applause,

                        dubeity, clinking of ice tea glasses)

"not only must the team demonstrate continuous improvement
but sooner rather than later
                        it must demonstrate the capacity to win,"
said Rosa Smith,
                Superintendent of City Public Schools
in her annual state of the district address.

                The district
        meets 5 of 27 state standards,
"far short of the end zone."

★

DIVERSITY SEMINAR

Blondie's very cute, just can't help it.

Don't you play that game with me—
our teacher squelches her. And soon

news-hour tears drench Blondie's cheeks.

Teacher works up a young man:
indignation roiling him,   he speaks

centuries, nightmares, skin flinching
at history's whips.

By now even the spreadsheet guys
are boohoo's and aaaaah's.

Heads bent, they wobble back to
the relief of sedans in the parking lot.

And Teacher, who'd begun with children,
who's been fired, assaulted, fire-bombed,

rams her SUV through leaden snow
hurrying to another session,

her face dreamless,
unhistoricized.

★

Could it be the same one I saw in my mother's yard on a brilliant morning when my skin was the skin of childhood, the air the air of childhood? A dove stepping on the red dirt of childhood, the same elegant curves (damsel! damsel!), a shape we trace toward a nameless desire. The same hunted dove pointing toward shade and water. An equanimity arrives as if it had crawled out of a window, glad to be found, as if I am the rain puddle water that freshens its wings.

IV.

Colley worked in the plant until the early 80's,
suffers from chronic bronchitis,
                              chronic fatigue, hair loss,
rashes, and connective tissue problems,
had 3 tumors removed,
                    a hysterectomy.

   Ah, the purple sensationalisms of dismay . . .

To raise funds for struggling telecom company
McCaw sold Tatoosh
                    for $100 million.
Three hundred-foot yacht carries   2 helicopters,
40-foot speedboat,   sailboat,   swimming pool.

   No rest on the slate plateaus . . .

Removed from their care
                    by Child Protective Services

then returned by jury,
        the child was found bloody and unconscious.
He had broken legs and arms,
        bruises on his face, burns on his back.

No walk on the rope of paradox . . .

                Significant levels of plutonium present
in nearby patch of ground.
Other sections are still in use.

V.

Finding the subject, purely for poetry . . .

The ambassador faxes an invitation.
Three days later the FBI knocks.

Meanwhile, a grieving ensues:
married to a U.S. citizen for 15 years, father of 3,
Duruji is charged with defying
                        a deportation order 17 years ago.

In bus stations, airports,
                delivering for Meals on Wheels
not for rapture, but for belonging
                        and its bitter aftertaste.

Now, the woman on the next seat, in mid-flight,
smacks her child, stares you away.

What comes now to own our own at last, to end the story . . .

Cradling a storm, the Chair summons.
He wobbles to meaning, hits stride:

> *Why are they looking for you?*

Offers support.

★

At the dentist's office she was wearing a baseball cap, a wig, and sun-glasses she took off to read *People*. She had no eyebrows, her face looked sapped, the cheeks and chin cramped and relieved only by twitching. Then a nurse came into the waiting room. "Mrs. Colley, right this way please."

No, dear Peter, that's not how I knew her.

★

CAIRO IN THE MORNING

Concrete mixers grind, gravel trucks pouring loads.
Construction workers swap morning curses.

From her balcony, in a nightgown, a woman watches
the street. Not today, a hand waves, not this week.

A muezzin wails, others follow.
The city growls, regurgitating its beliefs.

Old taxis whir along, serenade walkers.
Trams lumber by. Maids line up for morning beans.

Teahouses fill; bus drivers, plumbers,
carpenters, clerks, the unemployed.

They eat falafel sandwiches, sip sweet tea
(an upward gaze), kiss both sides of their hands.

Dear Lord, Dear Lord,
there is little to love about the poor.

A white dog passes by, a cat's tail between its jaws,
a goat's horn tossed at my feet.

Peasant boys hawk tissue paper.
A leper girl sells jasmine sprigs.

And on the bridge an old cycler's body
covered with newsprint.

Little to love here, Lord.
Despite all effort, despite curiosity.

VI.

A paralysis
        lavished and lavished upon:
the difference between 'the poetry' and 'the pose.'

      The idea is to redeem the bourgeoisie . . .
      Are you up to the task?

Judge approves settlement involving
a car-dealership-owned van
                in a crash that killed 7.

Heart of Texas Dodge agrees to pay $300,000
to be divided among plaintiffs.

An old, indelible need rises under my skin.

I am in the old dusty bookshop, riveted
                by Joseph's dream,
the eleven brothers sliding under wolf skin—
and redemption:
      the tossed shirt heals
            Jacob's blind eyes.

A certainty attends me, a mad patience.

"As an electrician you got in there and crawl
over everything, everywhere pull motors from the plant
and take them to the shop for reconditioning . . ."

An American rage
                 and the attendant resignation.

INS want Duruji and wife Christine to provide proof
their children
               are actually Duruji's offspring.

A brief desolation. Undeniable
                like a stone in a shoe.

*

There are times, or among some lives, where there is no former self to reconstruct or even revisit. But that's not what you, Peter, meant by the necessity of a connection. And I suspect that's not why the dead you wrote about are still mere numbers. Perhaps that's why you're still horrified: the reports you received, and passed on, refused to bear names. And as they kept escalating, you began to see the bodies piling up, the mounds of them obstructing the horizon.

*

TEXAS IN THE AFTERNOON

Barley grass in winter, rude-boy lush,
and sweet pea seeds in my palm as if grains

of yeast, the same promise of ardor.

The neighbors' cat, lying on the carport floor,
flees,
        always jumping over the same spot in the fence.

I love her ritualized terror, her American sense of drill.
She sprawls behind the kitchen minutes later, asleep.

Midmorning grackles caw, the silver-blue mint
on their wings, a theft from the sun.

The live oak shading three front yards.
The squirrels store, lose and retrieve.

Exile,
       your ninety-nine names
trill the tip of my tongue.

Isn't it time to sing what I've gathered
into blessing—
              indigenous, though scant?

VII.

School officials apologize to a boy
                            forced to sit in a corner
for wearing a Steelers jersey on
                         Cleveland Browns spirit day.

The issue is artifice—coincidences arranged
          to connect what cannot be connected . . .

As a child, the alleged murderer,
                    Sapp,
was raped, tortured, burned, and cut.

He saw one of his brothers drown in a lake,
another set on fire.

He slashed a distinctive signature
                        on the girls
who were on their way
               to a neighborhood bakery.

After 2 hours, the boy,
                now in a Cleveland Indians t-shirt,
was allowed
          to return his desk to its normal position.

★

He used to come to our table, a big burly man with a ready, languorous laugh. His hand, when he offered it to be shaken, was something you wanted to squeeze like a stress cushion. The food was good and wholesome as always. And yes, we ate there because it was exactly what he delivered to the old, the sick, and the unpardonable.

VIII.

Through maples, quicksilver burnishes leaves.

It's the mind's work, this human universe.

Woman charged with first DWI is sentenced to 2 years.

And sadness beaming from a ragged star?

The eyes won't allow such revelation:
                                shades of self-love
that flower
           from an elaborate contempt.

Judge Hoague (63) says a drunk driver killed his mother.
It was the main reason he pursued a criminal justice career.

Vice squad officers have repeated
sexual encounters with prostitutes
                              they are investigating.

City council approves
                pay raise for chief of police.

IX.

To reach beyond the threshold, drafted by discovery:

fingerprints on fogged-up windows,
the heart's trace-lights
                    shadowing everything.

I tell the FBI agent I refuse to be an informant.

Sedition, the sweat on my blackened hands:
he asks to use the bathroom, to make a phone call.

Biography chirps through corn plains, along wires and leaves:
a pragmatical math beaming
                    into the stratosphere.

Chair wheezes relief.
Dean offers a continental shrug.

Library returns $36,293 of unused funds to be used
to increase working hours of city and county courts.

Why don't you just lay low,   make friends . . .

★

The world doesn't wait. A November morning, a rustle in the oak branches. And yes, Peter, there are hardships in the world, only so that we can imagine them. I bring my ear to the throbbing, I listen for the sudden rustling of her cells, the procession traversing her vessels. The hum is the constant exhale from the dark angel's lungs. The same puff blowing through the detention cell. His doughy hands, two doves resting on his sleeping torso. I look up from the new soil under me, and out of the oak a hawk emerges. It soars like a kite, a squirrel's tail dangling from its claws. My heart leaps, as I walk out to the street following it, running even, caught in an inexplicable and devastating joy.

*

From this far
              what we love most
is cause for urgency.

Yet you remain self-consumed.

I am certain that what I carry of you
is more wonderful
                    than I can know.

It's what makes me unknowable
when I look airline hostesses,
shop clerks, or janitors in the eye.

What's impossible to acquire

becomes merely amusing.

I walk around it—wistful—and proceed.

But toward what?

A whiff of you,

a face sketched on a napkin.

A song you hated, and I loved.

3.

ECHO & ELIXIR 4

The chain inside my chest winds itself up again.
I stand uncertain where the blessing lies.

The scents the air held fall and are soaked
by the dirt beneath my feet. A memory had flared.

My hair, tremulous, told the news of this day.
The satin hues now shoot back to the sun.

The cart rides off loaded with pink, ivory,
bright orange, royal blue bolts.

Now I press seeds in with my shoes.
And my father sends me to fetch

a bucket of sand from the nearby beach.
The cart had pulled to our store

in the Metalsmiths' Bazaar.
Now the language is late afternoon.

The cartman's bronze muscular arms,
his sweaty unshaved face, his tea-stained teeth.

What happens afterwards is the same.
A mocking bird's medley, the hum

of a two-lane highway I faintly hear.
I am only forgetting. Remember that

when you see me walking this field.
Bolts of satin wrapped in clear plastic,

on the labels, the image of a smiling Chinese
girl, red-cheeked, with short hair—,

multiplied, disappearing among the crowds.
Now the sweat on my face reads the breeze.

I had to visit another country to know
that the mule's scents were delicious.

I had to ask someone to understand how beauty
edged the gold puddle the animal left behind.

Maybe that's why I stayed young for so long.

Now a crackling of branches.
Maybe a crow returning from tattered fields.

I remain uncertain where the blessing lies—
the chain inside my chest—

the rapture, the release.

HOME FRONT

First I was bundled with rope
and stared at the sky.
There was a softness and aunts.
Aisha came and we wrestled
for tenderness and foam.
Years and years she twirled.
Then she became a dry well.
In the kitchen we embraced her knees
and she collapsed years into decades.

In the middle they begin punching,
small fists prying and tossing clumps.
He does not feel.
Can you reach the liver?
He does not hurt.
A girl saws open my bones
and sucks out the marrow
the way her great aunt does.
They want my brain smoked
and fried with eggs.
I say I'm tired, and a boy points a finger:
Beware goat!
Tomorrow we take out the intestines
and stuff them with herbs and rice.

And Ummi sits in the corner
and irons everyone's clothes.

Maisoona's eye drifts.
She sees through chipped glass.
She reads Batoota's travels

among the red skins of Russia
and Bengal's porcelain gods.
She wants to follow him
through tempests and seas,
rivers choked with moss.

On the edge of the bed
Ibrahim smokes,
the magazines
piled and read. At night
he writes his bride
pages upon pages of talk.

What do you think
of the man who calls in the afternoon?
Fatma wants to know
in case she marries him.

The officer at the checkpoint says:
Bring us back this bride
in not too many years.
Everyone laughs,
passports clutched in hand.
Maisoona blinks
her lazy eye past us,
past the border and its guards.

No one jumps in Jeddi's lap.
He is listening to a far off sound,
brother to music and pain.

Aisha's baby will not sleep
and I am a monkey and I am good.
A cat meows. Ibrahim barks.
Who did the zebra bray?
Please trumpet like an elephant.
Please, please the owl's hoot.

CRICKET MOUNTAIN

The bridge under our wheels moaned, some said, because it was built in a time of war. Others were more specific—it moaned because of the two men buried in the concrete. Rommel built it, the British maintained the asphalt after he was driven away. My father drives across it with the car lights off. The haze from the city is enough to show the way, he explains. We stop by a channel that carried sea water to the salt fields. There are no birds, not even the sudden flop of a fish, or the rumble of the city's thousand pariahs that roamed the streets and howled through the night. The sound of the crickets crawls like a creature wanting to be noticed, yet is quick to withdraw. My father rests his hand on my shoulder to quiet me. Soon there is nothing in the world but the crickets' hum, an ordered machinery, a vibrating zone. You feel the air shiver around you, the sound wrapping you like a shroud. If you close your eyes, you can almost see the mass of their history, the design of their invention, and the idea of their purpose. Then this heap of intangibles rises like a mountain of silver, glittering, luminous, doing away with the dark.

Who was I then, and who was my father?

And what was that city that tangled us in its muddy streets?

ECHO & ELIXIR 5

Maybe love is a walk to astonishment.
Or a ship stranded on the shore of oblivion.
The infinity in the atom,
the treasures found in a word from long ago, now retrieved,
and the mind's chamber so luminous
it sees nothing but you.

Soul of my heart and my eyes' lanterns.
My loved one's hair is tangled
like a tumble weed, soft as down.
My gazelle and the music in her walk.
My freckled wonder. My apricot.

Maybe these are the heart's cymbals that guide its trance:
Rouhi. Gharami. Ishqi. Ahla ayami.
Maybe to say "I love you"
in another language
is not to love you at all.

Hear me say it, *Habibti.*
I say: *N'hibik.*

GENEALOGY OF FIRE

My sister held an old piece of bread.
She pointed to the fungus growing on it
and told my mother
"This is how we began."
My mother was a planet
in search of an explanation,
and my sister an idea
hoping to plant itself in the dirt.
As you can imagine
they didn't get along too well.

If I were to say
take these embers and carry them
in your hands,
use a rag for help . . . would you?
Let's not hypothesize,
and ask for feats that happen without volition.

An astrologer in Arabic is a *falaki*.
He or she watches stars swim in the *falak*.
And *falak* is the word for star
                    for orbit
                              for sky.
So my sister worries about her children.
She spanks them,
hates to hear them criticized.
They are orbits, stars, heavens.
And if that is motherhood, and because
a woman gets into her white car
and the world is full of white cars
and they always disappear like comets

on unfathomable orbits,
birth must be a machine
that braids chance and bird call,
a wave on whose fluctuations
street sounds and mysteries float.

I was born in a hot country,
hot most of the time. Dusty.
The water tasted of salt
and the sun turned our skins
into the color of fading bruises.
In the winter the rooms were cold
and we slept under many blankets
and huddled when we were awake
and blew breath into our hands
when teachers hit us with their bamboo sticks.

My sister's daughter
tosses her book aside.
A budding galaxy,
a swirl of centuries of ecstasy and torment,
she no longer wants to be
the next Simone Weil.
"I shall put on flesh," she declares,
the refrigerator handle in her grasp.

When my mother is alone in a room
she begins rocking.
When she does not know the answer to a question
she rocks three times.
When she falls asleep she curses

all those who make more than breathing sounds.
Night is long in her night,
the day a sickle,
the moon high high, and rain
eventually destroys a man's house
who has nothing but a cat that meows.

My sister's school was named after a holy woman.
The first wife of the prophet.
The classrooms were the prophet's tears.
Weep with me now that I have children
who have grown thin and tall like irises,
like corn stalks. Winds will blow at them
and the world will choke them.
Varicose veins and late night laundry.
Sadness happily rendered penetrates their music,
an unarmed robber, a potter careful
about keeping the oven clean.

Sisterhood, daughterhood
and the myriad arabesques of water.
She saved her wage money,
all of it, and bought herself some land.
And if she were, and if they were
hast thou not seen how the day
peels itself from the dark
to wake in the swamps of night,
hast thou not seen how the moon wanders
traversing among her mansions,
the air cool and smooth as satin,
hast thou not seen her return like a withered branch

every dust mote a little star,
and if she were, and if they were
knowst thou not how we paired thee
to disappear like fog at sunrise
knowst thou not how we multiply thee
on crowded roads or dead gardens,
and still thou returneth to me a bare single soul
and if her voice, and if their voices
were to be swallowed by the sounds
peace unto me the day I was born
of forests or shifting dunes,
peace upon me the day I die
how will I console the world?
the day I am raised . . .

ECHO & ELIXIR 6

She was our neighbor, the diabetic woman who kept having children. Please send us new photos, they said. Two cousins went to jail and one died under torture. Rafaa goes to Alexandria once a year to remember his joyful youth. His friend was being beaten by a gang, and to defend him, your nephew stabbed one of them in the shoulder. Her third child's right arm ended at the elbow. The old house is now empty, not sure whether to sell it or tear it down. Your brother has an ulcer and burps all day long. Don't worry about grammar, just send us letters. Father came back from London in excellent health, looked like a bridegroom. Her second child was born without a left hand. Your poor sister is balding, too many male hormones. Her first one had a finger missing. His wife now says, how come no one told me about this, and everyone goes *he he he*. And the fourth had two fingers protruding out of his left shoulder, no arm. She was our neighbor, the diabetic woman who kept having children. His friend was being beaten by a gang and your nephew stabbed one of them. Please send us new photos, they said. Father came back from London in excellent health. Her second child was born without a left hand. The third's right arm ended at the elbow. And the fourth had two fingers protruding out of his left shoulder, no arm. Your brother has an ulcer and burps all day long. His wife now says, how come no one told me, and everyone laughs and laughs. Your poor sister is balding, too many male hormones. Her first one had a finger missing. Two cousins were jailed, one tortured to death. Don't worry about grammar, just send the damn letters. Rafaa goes to Alexandria to relive his joyful youth. She was our neighbor, the diabetic woman who kept having children.

SELIMA!

My cousins had a parrot. He called only the name of one girl. Whenever the parrot called her name, he would close his eyes and roll his neck as if to swallow or to clear his blue throat. I would run to the kitchen to bring him peanuts which he ate slowly and deliberately, the ones he picked from my palm clicking against the insides of his black mouth. I would then plead with him, calling out my cousin's name. But the parrot would look past me as though the call took him too by surprise, a burden he had to suffer, a noise that had come from a house now hopelessly shut.

The parrot was never named and that may explain why no one mentions him now. The girl whose name he called married years ago and fought her husband through two pregnancies, but did not divorce. Sometimes when she cooks his meals, she begins to feel a dull hate tighten a fist inside her. When this happens, my cousin sets out on her own. She walks carefully to avoid stepping on hedgehog carcasses or wild artichoke spikes. She looks at the ground for snake and scorpion tracks, listening for the wild wolf-dogs that lurk on the outskirts of the city. She walks for hours to sit under a poinciana, to dip her feet in the stream that sometimes runs past the house deep in the lost parrot's heart.

ON APPLES AND SHEPHERDS

A shepherd herding his father's flock,
twenty when he tasted apples
for the first time. He bites into a hint of cedar,
brittle mountain air, spring water
and fibrous flesh colored sunlight,
green vessels lining wood and speckled red skin,
the climate of another country
streaming between his teeth.

To live in London then years later,
to speak the English of Mallarmé,
to *for* the "to,"
which the "where,"
to walk through a haze of language
senses gloved, and time surrendering
to the present tense.

But O the air and its latitudes!
Pockets the mind can slip into.
O to have smelled so many things!
An apple in the coarse hand of a shepherd.
A house by a channel where
a buffalo carcass stinks up the world.
You open a door and the air
is a cloud of frankincense.
You stand at a traffic light
and a bus blows its black flags,
Tripoli, circa 1968.
You cough then faint.
And years before in a warehouse,
a jug of acid breaks open

and you smell your arms burn.
Henna on your wife's hands.
Cigarette smoke
from your daughter's room.
You tell her you'll break her fingers.
Beer on your son's breath.
You say nothing . . . because, because . . .
Fire in your pension.
And this morning you walk to your car,
February air, you breathe out
in clouds. Spruce,
the green of evergreen.

Satellites feed you a hundred channels.
You flick through a thousand kissing scenes.
And the hours that eat into your waiting
for life, to do what? The children,
the work, the air that keeps running
past the reach of your lungs.
Drift now, drift again
to the day you lost a son to August.
You smelled words, some solicitous,
some enigmatic, pure air.
The boy lay dead on the street,
the runaway driver never found.
The smell of your loss: metallic.
The smell of rage: wet, dead leaves.

Lord of shepherds,
Lord of jasmine and airplanes,
excrement and drive-throughs.

Lord of tarmac and the frenzied passing of time.
Lord of basil and wild sage,
apples and diesel fumes,
and whatever splits the soul like a pod.
Forgotten days, out now,
bats at the break of day.
We are pages
miles away from the river,
the bean field, the cracked heels,
years away from the book.

I look at a map, the city where I live,
a desk, a salary, a phone.
I run to her, a diver coming up for air.
A lover on the other side of the continent.
The citrus smell of earth.
There is no end to this.

There is no end to this either.
Somewhere within your vision animals graze.
You pull at a shoot and chew at a thought.
It feels you've never gotten up from here:
you light a lamp
in a house at the edge of a field,
(a hint of frankincense)
always facing the same mystery:

the meal you sit to alone,
the life you swiftly cut up and eat.

4.

TUNED

He sits in front of the set
        blocking the view
   and the second sermon he catches

is the Arab Republic of Syria's live
        from the Ommayad Mosque—
   And when Egypt's Mufti amens

his final prayer—
        Thank you Lord for our sustenance—
   he steps into a long walk with God

to hear his fourth
        in the neighborhood mosque

*

        But oh the unheard-of raspberry jam!

and the tart made with pears
        we thought were potatoes
   as we watched—coat hanger

inserted in antenna slot—
        Halim, Cairo's Nightingale
   and Magda's bosom heaving

for breath, taken by
                    the honey-eyed Sharif—
          Then eventually someone

superimposed by a transmitter,
                    radiating in all directions
          travels the carrier waves,

breaking diplomatic blockades
                    empowered by relay stations,
          his movements amplified, arrives

descending the coat-hanger's
                    bent spine, his voice taking
          a short cut to sound reception plates

his grizzled image (his brown teeth
                    real, not a make-up trick) zipping
          through cathodes, anodes, triodes

to be smithereened by
                    the electron gun—Assembled
          at last, he looks us in the eye

grabs someone's collar and shouts
                    "What do you mean?"
          Someone raises eyebrows

in fury threatening revenge—
                    A village mayor twiddles
          a moustache signaling "kill"

★

We'd be sleeping in
                Friday mornings when he
        catches his first sermon

received via Samsung dish
                live broadcast from Dubai
        years after
                "Look here, man

Poke it with a fork"—
                an image from a pirate channel—
        the waves blocked by hills

buildings or towers, arrested
                by still air or calm seas
        bouncing back and forth

arriving as ghosts of
                original signal, and we now
        possessed beyond hope—

quantum theory a vague rumor
                in our books—glued—
        the outcome barely visible:

overpowered by the revolution's new cadre
                spooning cans of Patriotic pudding
        the salad, domestic (subsidized)

cucumbers and tomatoes
                    (unfortunately) from Crete—
            the cans littering Martyrs' Square

★

Frozen meals and the sun falling down
                    the apartment complex in dinnertime hush

        TELL HIM TO SHUT UP—
Evening silhouettes cross window frames
                    in the blue light of American loneliness

        SWITCH IT OFF, SWITCH IT
                                    OFF, I SAID

★

A fake blonde tempts Son of the Land, but
                    with difficulty, up elevator of money
            down staircase of moral rectitude—

He gets a late model Mercedes
                    an apartment in Heliopolis, but
            his heart is moping for Neighbors' Girl—

Then a small lunch follows, pills
                    for hypertension, angina, drops
            in his cataracted eyes while

Arabsat at an altitude
                    of thirty five thousand
            and eight hundred kilometers

on a geosynchronous orbit
                    relays "No more bloodshed"
            blaring live from Algiers—

But that wasn't it—
                    the imam raising skinny skyward arms—
            that wasn't the lump that throbbed in our throats

★

Son of the Land meanwhile
                    thinking thinking thinking
            smoking Rothmans and thinking—

of aunt Salma, the spinster
                    God bless her soul, who baked
            magazine recipes, and we

never thankful enough, licked
                    her chocolate glaze and
            the unprecedented raspberry jam—

She died heartbroken—

      Moping, the Neighbors' Girl he left behind—

"You change that channel
and I break your hand"
      that's what she said—

a bowl of cream whipped in her lap

   ★

Aboto wa Kastelo
      Fat Sack and Twig
    Laurel and Hardy

and the *Neeauh Neeauh Neeauh*
      of Curly and Moe—
Casbro the friendly ifrit

"the unfortunate events in My Lai"
      and the sad eyes of Prince Sihanouk
broadcast from the American base—

my sisters waking up groggy
      —the tart made with pears
we mistook for potatoes—

Then in a small southern town
        after Folgers and Sara Lee cake
    Grady and Aunt Esther

Diff'rent Strokes for diff'rent folks
        And Harry Reisner
    framed by the suspense of *tick*

tick tick tick tick tick
        not far from Central Bank
    tossing soft ones to Comrade Commander—

A year later *Newsweek*
        calling him the most dangerous
    man in the world—

I think it's the big one, Lamont—
        Watcha talkin' about—
    and that's the way it is

*

No CNN then, no Sky
        despite brand new crossbar
    backbone spiked with thorn-like

dipoles of various lengths
        despite directors, reflectors
    despite rotating base—

Not even Malta—Hold it still, hold it still—Larry
                Curly and Mo arriving wilted and soggy
         slipping right off the screen

★

Of course, it would comfort
                to think—that as he bent—
         his eyes fixed on the anchorman's—

that he'd known—
                or as he watched the imams—
         those tears—

the remote slipping from his hand—
                were in spite of what he'd known—
         and that he'd watched—

blocking the view—
                it would comfort to think—
         only to know what lay ahead

★

Algeria, Algeria,
            you big dick man—
        I can't wait to see you

★

To orders of Comrade Commander—
            tubs of rice dripping with fat
        the salad (domestic) cucumbers

and tomatoes (unfortunately) from Crete—
            the generation of inevitable victory
        danced, pumped fists, "Shit and Spit

on the enemies of Our Motherland!"

            "Following orders and protecting borders"
        that's what they said

★

Poor Father Bureaucrat—tearful flute
            or violin—has nothing to leave for
        Neighbors' Girl because there were

promises and the drama
> *of scowls and eyebrows*
and she

SWITCH IT OFF
> because of
their vast negligence and their bombs

eventually, carouses with
> pot-bellied schemers/contractors/
packaged meat manufacturers/

heroin dealers/
> real-estate tycoons—

> *Now stay tuned as we follow Son of the Land*

because
> *Not deaf, your eyes were . . .*
> SWITCH IT OFF FOR GOD'S SAKE

regularly played by Nour Sharif

> *I am with you as before*

(no relation to previous Sharif)

with you, with you as before—
> accounting major, job-less
smoking local cigarettes

＊

Still he watched the news
            his face close to the anchorman's
      as if he wanted to be kissed—

Swerving around his back
            in homes, schools, cafés—
      April dust coating every ledge—

Comrade Commander viewing
            the spectacle from a third floor
      window at Central bank

the bodies swinging—
            April dust settling on their lips—
      someone signaling "kill"

＊

The screen a shadow mask
            a layer of opaque materials
      covered with slots and holes—

An oracle, a premonition—
            In a small Southern town
      I gave you—five across your lips—

I broke your adolescent night
                    Earl Campbell and Mean Joe Green

TELL HIM TO SHUT UP

The screen, a shadow mask
                    when you sink into your . . .
          beaming dots

at eleven, twenty four, thirty three

SWITCH IT OFF—PLEASE SWITCH IT OFF
          I gave you Chico and the Man

The squalor of victory
                    ennui of defeat—
          I gave you the bombing of Baghdad

★

Then ten of them walk out—the speed
                    of electromagnetic radiation invariant—
          You see the reception—Hold it still—

We watched their thrashing—
                    Frequency the number of times
          a wave oscillates—

grunts from tangled limbs—
    a wire to speakers to transmit sound—
  the ferrite reverberating inside—

coils wrapped in translucent sheets—
    the ferrite concentrating energy—
  the coil inducing reception—

close-ups of abysmal vaginas—
    waves pushing the current on—
  copious overflows—

 ★

Still, he was planted in front of the set
    blocking the view—as if waiting
  for leopard-skin leotard—

long addicted to good scotch by now—
    Poor Father Bureaucrat's daughter—
  the Neighbors' Girl he left behind

 ★

But—he saw us—caught
                not just by the beams
        but everywhere—

Tunisia, Tunisia—
                I am dripping, ya habibi—
        when are you gonna come—

on the curb
                of an endless evening—
        muscles twitching to

Morocco, my gazelle—
                Don't you love me?
        I'm still waiting for your call—

twitching to someone signaling—
                shoulders collapsing when
        the credits roll—

a commercial break—
                the remote kicks a second wind
        into a patient deferral, well honed

★

Then something happens
                not just the switch to foreign cigarettes
        and Kenny G, not even—

Hold it still, poke it with a fork—
                (that was much later)
      an Aristotelian coincident:

someone walks by a mosque
            and hears the tearful-organ-
      hopeless-flute theme

or the police catch a whiff
            and follow it all the way
      to the Quranic recitation:

the best

        dear viewer
   we can end our night on

★

In seconds—
        OUT OUT O
     BAT OF NIGHT

confirmed to a million strangers—
           the blossoming sabras of rage battering
      the ether, emptying streets—

what took months to believe—
           That's when someone grabs . . .
      What do you mean?

The fake blond is there too
             smacks her companion, gets
       smacked back harder

her real Versace sunglasses
             flying, break—
       And the Son of the Land

and Neighbors' Girl—
             Police chief takes time from
       busy schedule to attend their wedding feast

★

But you—the flames
             lapping vinyl siding—
       ice cream on a lip—

the firemen's water soaking
             burned furniture and books—
       How they

on that slow Saturday—
             Morning Fire Destroys Home
       in Skyview Hill

A Tragedy in Cedar Brook—
             wanted your hot tears!
       But you, a foreigner—

a throwback to *camera-shy*—
                          some tradition giving you dignity—
              refusing—

your final answer—
                          to play the nation's daily
              catharsis game

★

The young couple, Mercedes sold
                          in favor of locally made Nasr—
              her hair dyed natural color—

are sent off to their Shobra high rise—
                          (older sister blushing at
              Brother Police Chief's proposal)—

And they showed us the cut
                          fingers, passing electric current
              the pulse translated by the tuner

rendering swollen faces—
                          OUT OUT O BAT OF NIGHT—
              the cigarette burns, the frizzling

forced confessions, the torturers—
                          Shit and Spit—
              emission and absorption of radiation

occurring in finite units of energy
            the nervous judge, the rag tag
        firing squads, the bodies—O BAT OF NIGHT—

matter exhibiting duality
            of wave and particle, the bodies—
        No last flight

★

The smell of Folgers and the sun
            breaking through
        dawn light hush

O thicker than the Ocean and the Gulf—

            O you that births double your worth—

    O you of long walks with God—

The camera's prisms
            and mirrors sought you—
        in a small southern town as I broke—

five across your lips—
            the camera lens focusing
        light from the flames—

And when the king of Morocco offers—
        to produce a continuous image—
    numerous times per second—

his hand for the Supreme Mufti—
        Thank you Lord of our daily sustenance—
    the mysterious pear tarts

and the unheard-of raspberry jam—
        the Mufti to kiss (Samsung dish
    rattled by trade winds now)

in the Grand Mosque facing the sea—
        The eyes collapse, head falls—
    the children aching for Mondial:

Scotland losing to Peru—
        grandchildren for Scooby Doo—
    the remote slipping from his hand—

5.

ECHO & ELIXIR 7

The stories you believe are the stories you make.

So one enters a room alone.
People there and they see the dust
and they hear the echo of travel.

They remember distances and songs,
they read a script that befuddles the page:
trains, airports, short-term leases,

hawkers and dingy bars.
They see windstorms and sandstorms,
ghost towns and customs shacks.

But that is not why I keep thinking
one life is not enough
or that I've lived enough.

It is not why I think
the present is a blockade on
the intersection of the future and past.

It is not why
my boredom is resourceful,
why it finds me wherever I go

or why I feel that somewhere else
in the infinite bend below the horizon
better things are happening,

events and lives that pertain to me.

It is not the reason
I love you and love you,

and leave us both aghast.

AT THE COLUMBUS ZOO WITH
GOETHE IN POCKET

They devour, nibble,
yawn when satisfied.
Stand, look at them,

the sky behind you
flaps her wings.
You are a signatory

ennobled by submission.
This is the sway
where every subject grazes,

a sphere made sublime
by its question.
The sun a howl,
the clouds a hunger,

your freedom is weighed
in steps now,
the law ahead
a watchful horizon.

NOCTURNES ON EVOLUTION
& CATASTROPHE

This is not a dream:

I wheel him out of the hospital building
(the nurse grimacing at our disregard for rules)

to the back terrace from where
we can see the distant hills,

their silhouettes a wavy ribbon separating
city lights from the glow of a full moon.

His eyes are pretty much gone now;
still, I position him to face it

as if he could feel its pull,
as if it could stir a tide within him.

He leans his head back (and, yes, watches)
allowing the dull sheen to shower him,

a nostril flaring in recognition of the July air
purified by the firs surrounding us.

I light a cigarette, and he says something
like *who's there*, or *put it out*.

When I turn to catch his words
his body appears like an X -ray of itself,

the rib cage (a caricature of)
two alien hands about to clasp fingers

around the stutter of his heart.
And downwards, toward the abdomen

where the pain taking him rested,
a glow, an abandoned fire.

★

A month earlier, I stepped out of Ziryab
with two friends to Central Street

past the bright clothing stores, shawarma stands,
internet cafés and cell phone shacks.

Murad, who'd filled the night
with Pushkin and Chekov,

more erudite with every sip of arak,
led us forward with another monologue

down a slope that loosened my bones
in the cool of a June moonlight.

And Annas, who for years had walked past a sign
prematurely "saluting" his martyrdom

was forgetting to caress his torso
in his constant dressing of a wound,

an intifada bullet earned eight years ago.
We both chanted following Murad's lead,

God is great!
God is greater than Tagore!

thankful for the arak, the magnificent sky,
the kanafeh syrup still sticky on our hands.

But soon at a ledge overlooking the valley
where Ramallah's suburbs lay, we stood

transfixed gazing toward the new settlements,
their pinkish lights, golden caps

stoppling the highest (strategic) hills.
Annas rested his hand on his scar now

and told of how he and his friends
stoned the soldiers, and how easy

heroism was, finding time meanwhile
to chat up the girls who brought them stones

daring their families' rebuke,
and how, yes happy, he'd felt

even as the bullet (rubber-coated)
tore through his side, the operation

to save him taking eight hours
and half his intestines with it.

"That's how we spent our days," he said.
"But at night, after the soldiers

and newsmen withdrew, the settlers came
to our village their Uzis cocked,

roamed our lanes, cussed us in Arabic
daring us to come out. Our houses clammed up

in silence, our lights dimmed,
and we ducked or ran past our windows

cursing the moon when it rose full
and betrayed us. They came to wipe out

what we'd gathered through the day.
And we rushed out with dawn light,

burned tires and threw stones
to rekindle it, retrieve it."

*

Rain falls on the waves,
the sky reminding the sea:

This is how I made you.

And the lover tells the beloved
"I loved you first. I held the first thread

tied the first knot, my love the weaving.
I wove on though my fingers were unraveling,

though I was ceasing to be.
When you were complete, I'd vanished.

You are this exultance, this circle
spinning and naming the emptiness."

/

The rain is a note of grief,
a bird astounded by parting.

For days it called, "Are you there?"
and for days no one said, "Here I am."

Whitman's bird, Whitman's mother
fretting, waiting for the squaw's return,

and Tagore's Amal staring from the window,
dying in wait for the mail.

/

"Each window offers its view,"
                                    a wise aunt told me.
"You can't switch them around."

"Each day peels its gifts,"
                            a family friend said.
"You can't exchange them."

You and I, two windows, each
allowing its breeze into the room.

We let the dust gather on ledges.
We let the papers blow all over the floor.

We knew what we were doing.
We knew what was needed to be done.

We heard the bird call
and looked at each other.

We heard the rain
answer in dissipating notes.

We closed our eyes
to listen harder, to make certain.

And when I opened my eyes, Father,
you'd disappeared.

And when you opened yours, Father,
I was gone.

*

In Pforzheim, after I put him to bed,
I go on a walk and get lost.

I wander for an hour, but
there is no one to ask, no taxi in sight.

Then from a bar, four young men
step out, raucous, obviously drunk,

two of them with shaved heads.
I avoid their eyes.

After three blocks, they fall silent
and still walk behind me.

After I take a right turn
their footsteps thud closer,

and after another turn
they seem at my heels.

I duck into a side street (bad idea)
and begin to run

then jump into someone's yard,
walk to the back fence, climb

into another house, then another, slide
behind a gooseberry bush lining the fence,

and sit on the ground and wait.

My heartbeat, though mine,
its rhythm is older.

I hear my terror and its echo, a cadence
of second-guessing arguing that

my swiftness is not instinct,
but choreography. Yet how natural,

like being caught in a rain shower,
it seems. Even my pursuers

sound like actors caught in a drama
they can't improvise their way out of.

I stay put, and can't help,
an hour later, but reach for the berries

(succulent, not yet sweet)
a sour prayer, my inevitable deviation.

★

Now here's the dream.

From the bathroom's open door, I see her
ease in through the window.

Late summer out, February in the dream,
I dream that I am sleeping.

She enters as if footless,
stands at my bedside a second

then slips under the comforter,
softly nudges me to hold her.

And when I do, and when I take her
fully and completely into my arms,

I feel a stab slice through my back,
painful, sudden. Words

or some other horde begin
to crawl out of my spine like moths

and rise to hover above me.
Then she slips away wafting off

through the window, the drizzle
that hung above following her

like the tail of a comet's core.
She was a short woman, dark-haired—

a fairy, I am told later by an interpreter—
who'd breezed in and out

of people's dreams for millennia.

But no one could divine the shadow

who wore my clothes and sat on the chair
beside the dresser watching everything,

and who then got up, faceless,
pulled the dagger from me,

showed me the crested handle, nodded
unsurprised by the bloodless blade.

EMERSON REVISITATION

Death and progress
conjoin on the tongue's
amnesia. The fantasy:

a suspension: May's hot
noons and cool nights
a torsion wheel.

We come to witness
our dispossession. We come to
hear the scales of survival.

The leaves' spillage: glory.
The unsorrowful gaze:
a decomposing wren.

Deeper into the mind's
parched distance: the raspy note
that sounds the nothingness.

DARK ANTHEM

Sometimes I look at them
    like treasures I hid in a box.
I walk out stealthily—
    I can't tell anyone I'm going—
and soon I raise my arms
    as if I'd peeled layers
and layers of cloth or lifted
    piles of heaped carpets,
my fingers loose but firm,
    picking the air's locks,
unchaining a miracle from the dark,
    a herd of small animals,
a handful of albino moths,
    a flock of doves I release
that take off and gyrate
    then settle in the trees
because they cannot bear
    leaving me.

        Sometimes,
walking with friends I say
    "Look at them." Look,
how they glow, how
    they nod, it's they not us,
who are spectators. They are
    the tribe's children gathered
to meet the strangers and cheer
    our caravan's arrival.
They peep at us from every corner,
    try to see us naked,
ogling us as we eat, surprised
    by our fingers, our nails,

our primate hair. And when
      we look at them, they giggle
and run away, only to stare
      at us again from behind
their mothers' dark thighs.

      But what have we brought them?
It's then that I begin
      naming: I hold the hand
of the generous one, I mess up
      the artist's hair, I shake
with affection the strong one's
      shoulders, I pinch the sad one's
cheeks, I caress the paunch
      of the glutton—our cook of course—,
and kiss the lips of the beautiful
      and brag licking mine.
I embarrass them, and I
      embarrass myself, half drunk,
my head a song, gagging
      on a thought larger than
my body can contain.

      Tonight though, they
are the glint of salt
      spilled on dark linoleum,
unashamed, mute hefts,
      lugging matter. They're death
in the distance, the long walk,
      a bee line to naught—
the sailor in cold waters,

the ship's metal moaning,
bubbles stirred into froth
        around an insatiable hole.
Freezing, he sees a shimmer
        of a lighthouse beam,
and though his mouth is full
        only of a wet curse for God,
and though his mind has spilled
        all its thoughts like a sack
of coins suddenly punctured—
        O Mother's forgiveness,
Father's stubbly chin,
        Sister's last kiss, Brother's
embrace, the mouth exclaiming
        milk teeth, the lips
that reluctantly come to love—,
        the gold pieces clink
and bounce like fire flies.
        Amidst this, he turns
for one last glance
        and what he sees sinks him.
Nothing he can do now,
        nothing he can be now
is of use to anyone.

        Loved one
    sleeping two oceans away,
loved one sleeping in my bed,
        two moons in your sky,
two moons nesting on
        your shoulders, that which growled
meekly, skittered and hid,

            a mere punctuation
of a day, lies sprawled,
            its myriad eyes feeding
on their orbits lighting
            the way in which they will dissolve.
What now, dear grass?
            Dear hills, dear silent houses,
your blue hues dimmed.
            What of this that bears down
heavy and comfortable as a pet
            and the sad years I've fed it?
What now, rosemary bush?
            your oil rubbed on my skin
and I am fragrant as a mosque
            during Eid. The late hours,
walking famous cities
            holding her hand, float about me,
autonomous even when
            cupped in the mind's hold.

To raise an arm out then,
            and up, to discern what it can
carry beyond its dimensions
            out of the soul's shell,
is a feeble attempt at attention.
            For soon the whole place
will be encased in the bubble
            of daylight. Sometimes I think
I'd be satisfied if I were only
            a body nosing the ground,
unaware of the canopy as it unfurls,
            and as daylight becomes

a childhood theater in summer,
          its ceiling open, and I see
the film—a Mexican Western—
          and look up again
at the sky and at them, alternating
          between two realities,
both ephemeral, though one
          fictional and more heroic
and the other cutting through
          light years to reach me
with a cold, sharp nudge.

          The soul, I must have learned then,
was that bifurcation,
          always arriving unanticipated
like an animal drooping
          with fatigue or giddy shaking
a proverbial tail, or with
          dark-eyed sorrow
dismembering time, seducing
          us again with possibility.
It is then that I abandon
          my eyes, my bearing witness
a gesture of begrudging tolerance.
          Yet the hand aches
responding to a hunger beyond
          hunger, emerging from a core
beyond experience. And what
          it plucks from the sky
is never untainted, never
          unearthly, and I am reminded
of a childhood tale: the Bedouin,

          facing starvation
reaches for the leather amulets
          bearing his god's name,
and eats them. All his strictures
          now collapsed by, or into,
one pure certainty.

                    It's too late
          to hope for such purity,
and I'm wise enough not
          to be enthralled by the idea
of a clean victory over
          what I know to be a deferral,
a process we instigate to silence
          the whirlpool of possibilities
spinning below, because
          the happiness at hand is pictorial,
static, a plaque on a wall,
          earned in collateral, always
arriving as anti-climax.
          And the past is something to recover,
or to recover from,
          horizontal, iconographic
like the spot where
          the rope walker starts his walk.
His stability on the rope
          is all that matters, and the future
is an arrival into safety
          that will wrap him in brooding
as soon as he reaches it.

I think I keep coming here
because there's no arrival,
        and if I were to fall,
there would be no rescue,
        because there was no damage
to begin with, borne as I am
        like a breath, naturalized
within my rib cage, essential
        only to the world
contained within my eyes.
        Still, I am magnetized
and pulled, shedding all
        I've merged into, surrendering
to a fear so awesome, it becomes
        ecstatic as it singes me.
This is how I carry myself
        back to you. Under
porch light you'll find
        me tenuous as star dust
as I reach for the mist
        of your breath to anchor me,
for the rub of your touch
        to render me mortal and resonant.

NOTES & ACKNOWLEDGMENTS

The title of this book comes from the following passage from Mana Ibn Shaqlouf's *Khalis Al-Ulum fi Urf Al-Nujum* (A Concise Treatise on the Laws of the Stars):

The Zodiac of Echoes is a system of divination based on a single galaxy consisting of five planets that rotate around a speckled sun. One planet, *Maradh Al-Qulub* (heart sickness), distinguished by its crimson color and rosy swirls, informs on the seeker's state of love. Another, a greenish planet with variations of gray and yellow hues, is consulted on issues of bloodlines and potency. It is called *Nour Al-Ansal* (light of lineage). The third planet, *Saf'hat Al-Dhamir* (the scroll of the soul) is a solid blue celestial body which appears in differing sizes depending on the questioner's condition. Its function, as the name implies, is to inform on the state of the soul. The fourth, a citrus colored sphere, is consulted on many matters that range from material wellbeing, the potential for war and peace, and on future weather conditions such as flood and drought. It is called *Kitab Al-Ashya* (the book of things). And finally, a bright small white planet, clear as milk or the petals of a daisy, is consulted on the interpretation of dreams or prophecies one acquaints and does not understand. When the thrust of the misunderstood phrases is good, the star shines in the aforementioned brightness; if the words are ominous and foreboding, the star appears with a yellow halo running along its edges. Called *Nashid Al-Maani* (the song of meaning), this sphere never appears alone. Like a child hanging on to its mother's skirt, it always attaches itself to one of the bigger planets. Some have suspected it to be a moon to all these planets, a highly unlikely claim. As to the speckled sun, named *Matahat Al-Amal* (the labyrinth of yearnings), it has been postulated, concurrent to our belief, that the speckles on the sun are prayers, human and otherwise, unable to proceed higher into the heavens. These prayers become attached to this sun that attracts them like a magnet. Since the whole zodiac is in constant motion, and as this sun constantly spins about its orbit, some prayers become detached. Unable to resume their original ascent to the highest tiers, the prayers spin about the zodiac filling it with their echoes. It is the mingled sounds of these unanswerable prayers that gives this zodiac its name.

Ibn Shaqlouf, a North African scholar (1156-1201), was born in Zlitin (in modern day Libya) where he studied with the town's Sufi masters. From there he went on to study at Al-Zaitouna in Tunis, then at Al-Azhar in Cairo where he was certified as a judge in both the Maliki and Hanafi traditions. It was in Cairo that he became interested in astrology which he studied on his own. *Khalis Al-Ulum* was written while the author traveled in India and where he eventually settled in Hyderabad. The passage above is a perfunctory description that Ibn Shaqlouf provides as part of a chapter about alternative astrological systems that markedly differ from the Egypto-Grecian horoscope system known in the West, and the Indian system that is also in practice today.

Thanks to the editors of the following journals for publishing earlier versions of these poems:

The Alembic: Vicinity "II, III, V, VI."
Artful Dodge: "Cricket Mountain," "Selima."
Banipal (London): "Dark Anthem."
Black Warrior Review: "Echo & Elixir 6."
Cultural Dynamics: "Tuned."
The Drunken Boat: "Echo and Elixir 4."
Faultline: "At the Columbus Zoo with Goethe in Pocket."
Grafitti Rag: "Cairo in the Morning" as "The City."
Indiana Review: Vicinity "IV, VII, VIII, IX."
The Kenyon Review: "Echo & Elixir 1," sections 1, 3, 5, 7 (published as 1, 3, 7, 11).
The Marlboro Review: "Texas in the Afternoon."
Mizna: "Diversity Seminar."
New England Review: "For Many Years I've Been Prohibited from Mentioning the Moon."

North Dakota Quarterly: "Home Front."
Paliaedes: "Rain Song," "On Apples and Shepherds."
Prairie Schooner: "Genealogy of Fire."
River Styx: "The Road from Biloxi," "Echo & Elixir 2."
Visions International: "Emerson Revisitation."

★

I wish to thank the Council for the Humanities at Princeton University for an Alfred Hodder fellowship, and The John Simon Guggenheim Memorial Foundation for an annual grant. Both were very helpful during the writing of this book. I am grateful to Talvikki Ansel, David Baker, Chris Green, David Kirby, Kurt Heinzelman, Salih Al-Moncef, and Ann Townsend, friends whose suggestions and criticism helped pull the book together. I am indebted, in time and attention, to David Wojahn, whose help was essential. Finally, I can never be grateful enough to Lisa Sanchez Gonzalez, whose encouragement and inspiration were a tremendous help in completing this book.

★

The poem "For Many Years I Have Been Prohibited from Mentioning the Moon" is for David Wojahn.

The poem "Rain Song" is after Badr Shakir Al-Sayyab's "Inshudat al-Mattar" (Rain Song). The poem includes several phrases from the original poem which are my translation. The italicized lines are based on Ahmad Rami's Arabic translations of Omar Khayyam's rubaiyat.

"The Wind" is for Jonathan Maskit, Barbara Fultner, Eliza Kent, and Maurizio Oliva.

In section I of the "Vicinity" sequence, the lines "Verily God hath not made a man/with two hearts in his chest" is verse 4 in Sura 33 of the

Quran. In section II, the line "until something human comes" is from Lucille Clifton's poem "leaving fox." In section III, the line "of rescue, to rescue" is based on a line from Lucille Clifton's poem "far memory." In section V, the line "to own our own at last" is from Lucille Clifton's poem "white lady."

In "Genealogy of Fire" some of the italicized sections toward the end of the poem are from the Quran, verses 13-14 in Sura 76, and verses 22–23 in Sura 22. The poem is for Halima Al-Bakoush and for Atta, Saniya, Aisha, and Nadia.

"Selima!" is for Naomi Shihab Nye.

"On Apples and Shepherds" is for Osama and Manal Muttawa.

In "Tuned" the phrase "tradition giving you dignity" is based on a line from William Carlos Williams's "For Elsie." "Tuned" is for George W. S. Trow.

"Nocturnes on Evolution and Catastrophe" is dedicated to the city of Ramallah, Palestine.

CPSIA information can be obtained
at www.ICGtesting.com
Printed in the USA
LVHW041126141218
600408LV00001B/4/P

9 781931 337168